W9-BBA-049

Wise Men Talking Series

CONFUCIUS

孔子说 Says

蔡希勤 编注

□责任编辑 韩晖

□翻译 赖波 夏玉和 郁苓

□绘图 李士伋

First Edition 2006
Third Printing 2009

ISBN 978-7-80200-211-1

Published by Sinolingua
24 Baiwanzhuang Road, Beijing 100037, China
Tel: (86) 10-68995871
Fax: (68) 10-68326333
Wedsite: www.sinolingua.com.cn
E-mail: fxb@sinolingua.com.cn
Printed by Beijing Songyuan Printing Co.Ltd.
Distributed by China International
Book Trading Corporation
35 Chegongzhuang Xilu, P.O. Box 399
Beijing 100044, China

Printed in the People's Republic of China

老人家说

Wise Men Talking

俗曰:“不听老人言,吃亏在眼前。”

老人家走的路多,吃的饭多,看的书多,经的事多,享的福多,受的罪多,可谓见多识广,有丰富的生活经验,老人家说的话多是经验之谈,后生小子不可不听也。

在中国历史上,春秋战国时期是中国古代思想高度发展的时期,那个时候诸子并起,百家争鸣,出现了很多“子”字辈的老人家,他们有道家、儒家、墨家、名家、法家、兵家、阴阳家,多不胜数,车载斗量,一时星河灿烂。

后来各家各派的代表曾先后聚集于齐国稷下学宫,齐宣王是个开明的诸侯王,因纳无盐丑女钟离春为后而名声大噪,对各国来讲学的专家学者不问来路一律管吃管住,享受政府津贴,对愿留下来做官的,授之以客卿,造巨室,付万钟。对不愿做官的,也给予“不治事而议论”之特殊待遇。果然这些人各为其主,各为其派,百家争鸣,百花齐放,设坛辩论,著书立说:有的说仁,有的说义,有的说无为,有的说逍遥,有的说非攻，有的说谋攻，有的说性善，有的说性恶，有的说亲非亲，有的说马非马，知彼知己，仁者无敌……留下了很多光辉灿烂的学术经典。

可惜好景不长，秦始皇时丞相李斯递话说“焚书坑儒”，结果除秦记、医药、卜筮、种树书外，民间所藏诗、书及百家典籍一把火烧个精光。到西汉武帝时，董仲舒又上了个折子，提出“罢黜百家，独尊儒术”，从此，儒学成了正统，“黄老、刑名百家之言”成为邪说。

“有德者必有言”，儒学以外的各家各派虽屡被扫荡，却不断变幻着生存方式以求不灭，并为我们保存下了十分丰富的经典著作。在这些经典里，先哲们留下了很多充满智慧和哲理的、至今仍然熠熠发光的至理名言，我们将这些各家各派的老人家的“金玉良言”编辑成这套《老人家说》丛书，加以注释并译成英文，采取汉英对照出版，以飨海内外有心有意于中国传统文化的广大读者。

As the saying goes, “If an old dog barks, he gives counsel.”

Old men, who walk more roads, eat more rice, read more books, have more experiences, enjoy more happiness, and endure more sufferings, are experienced and knowledgeable, with rich life experience. Thus, what they say is mostly wise counsel, and young people should listen to them.

The Spring and Autumn (722 – 481 BC) and Warring States (475 – 221 BC) periods of Chinese history were a golden age for ancient Chinese thought. In those periods, various schools of thought, together with many sages whose names bore the honorific suffix "Zi", emerged and contended, including the Taoist school, Confucian school, Mohist school, school of Logicians, Legalist school, Military school and Yin-Yang school. Numerous and well known, these schools of thought were as brilliant as the Milky Way.

Later representatives of these schools of thought flocked to the Jixia Academy of the State of Qi. Duke Xuan of Qi was an enlightened ruler, famous for making an ugly but brilliant woman his empress. The duke provided board and lodging, as well as government subsidies for experts and scholars coming to give lectures, and never inquired about their backgrounds. For those willing to hold official positions, the duke appointed them guest officials, built mansions for them and paid them high salaries. Those unwilling to take up official posts were kept on as advisors. This was an era when "one hundred schools of thought contended and a hundred flowers blossomed." The scholars debated in forums, and wrote books to expound their doctrines: Some preached benevolence; some, righteousness; some, inaction; some, absolute freedom; some, aversion to offensive war; some, attack by stratagem; some, the goodness of man's nature; some, the evil nature of man. Some said that relatives were not relatives; some said that horses were not horses; some urged the importance of knowing oneself and one's enemy; some said that benevolence knew no enemy... And they left behind many splendid classic works of scholarship.

Unfortunately, this situation did not last long. When Qin Shihuang (reigned 221 – 206 BC) united all the states of China, and ruled as the First Emperor, his prime minister, Li Si, ordered that all books except those on medicine, fortune telling and tree planting be burned. So, all poetry collections and the classics of the various schools of thought were destroyed. Emperor Wu (reigned 140 – 88 BC) of the Western Han Dynasty made Confucianism the orthodox doctrine of the state, while other schools of thought, including the Taoist and Legalist schools, were deemed heretical.

These other schools, however, managed to survive, and an abundance of their classical works have been handed down to us. These classical works contain many wise sayings and profound insights into philosophical theory which are still worthy of study today. We have compiled these nuggets of wisdom uttered by old men of the various ancient schools of thought into this series Wise Men Talking, and added explanatory notes and English translation for the benefit of both Chinese and overseas readers fond of traditional Chinese culture.

目录 CONTENTS

不患人之不己知〔10〕

Do not worry that your abilities are not appreciated. . .

不患无位，患所以立〔12〕

Don't worry about having no official position, but do worry about your ability to fulfill a post.

不义而富且贵，于我如浮云〔14〕

Ill-gotten wealth and rank are just like fleeting clouds to me.

不在其位，不谋其政〔16〕

Do not get involved in the government affairs that are not your responsibility.

D

大德不逾闲〔18〕

As long as one does not step out of bounds in big matters. . .

当仁，不让于师〔20〕

In the face of benevolence, do not give precedence even to your teacher.

道不同，不相为谋〔22〕

People who follow different political paths do not take counsel with one another.

道之以政，齐之以刑〔24〕

Regulated by the edicts and punishments. . .

德不孤，必有邻〔26〕

A man of virtue can never be isolated. He is sure to have like-minded companions.

弟子，入则孝，出则悌〔28〕

At home, a young man should be dutiful towards his parents. . .

F

发愤忘食，乐以忘忧〔30〕

The Duke of Ye asked Zi Lu about Confucius. . .

父母在，不远游〔32〕

When ones parents are alive, one should not go far away.

父母之年，不可不知也〔34〕

One must always keep in mind one's parents' birthdays. . .

富而可求也〔36〕

I would pursue wealth so long as it could be obtained legitimately.

富与贵，是人之所欲也〔38〕

Everyone desires money and high position. . .

G

工欲善其事，必先利其器〔40〕

A craftsman must prepare his tools beforehand in order to do his work well.

躬自厚而薄责于人〔42〕

Being strict with oneself and lenient to others is sure to save one from ill will.

古之言之不出〔44〕

In ancient times, people didn't say things lightly...

过而不改，是谓过矣〔46〕

Not to correct the mistake one has made is to err indeed.

过犹不及〔48〕

Going too far and not going far enough are equally bad.

H

好学近乎知〔50〕

To be eager to learn indicates wisdom because it may eliminate stupidity.

后生可畏〔52〕

Young people have great potential for achievements.

J

己所不欲，勿施于人〔54〕

Do not impose upon others what you do not desire yourself.

见善如不及，见不善如探汤〔56〕

Striving to be the first and fearing to lag behind. . .

见贤思齐焉〔58〕

When you meet a man of virtue, learn from him.

敬鬼神而远之〔60〕

If one respects the spirits of the dead and the gods. . .

君子不器〔62〕

A gentleman should not be like a utensil.

君子不以言举人〔64〕

A gentleman does not promote a man whose words are pleasant to his ear.

君子耻其言而过其行〔66〕

A gentleman takes it as a disgrace to let his words outstrip his deeds.

君子成人之美〔68〕

A gentleman helps others fulfill good deeds. . .

君子固穷〔70〕

When gentlemen become impoverished, they can still persevere in virtue.

君子和而不同〔72〕

A gentleman unites with people of principle and never follows others blindly.

君子谋道不谋食〔74〕

A gentleman devotes himself to studying the academic system of ideology instead of seeking food and clothing.

君子求诸己，小人求诸人〔76〕

A gentleman sets strict demands on himself while a petty man sets strict demands on others.

君子去仁，恶乎成名〔78〕

How can one be called a gentleman if one betrays benevolence.

君子食无求饱，居无求安〔80〕

A gentleman seeks neither a full belly nor a comfortable home.

君子坦荡荡，小人长戚戚〔82〕

A gentleman is always broad-minded while a petty man is always full of anxiety.

君子泰而不骄〔84〕

A gentleman always keeps even-tempered without being arrogant. . .

君子以文会友〔86〕

"A gentleman makes friends through his learning. . ."

君子忧道不忧贫〔88〕

What a gentleman worries about is not poverty but if there are right principles throughout the country.

君子有九思〔90〕

A gentleman concentrates on the following nine things. . .

君子有三戒〔92〕

A gentleman should maintain vigilance against three things. . .

君子欲讷于言而敏于行〔94〕

A gentleman should be careful in speech and quick to act.

君子之过也，如日月之食焉〔96〕

The gentleman's errors are like an eclipse of the sun and the moon. . .

君子贞而不谅〔98〕

A gentleman pays attention to faithfulness rather than small matters.

K

苛政猛于虎〔100〕

Tyranny is more cruel than a tiger.

克己复礼为仁〔102〕

One who restrains himself in order to observe the rites is benevolent.

L

老者安之〔104〕

I wish for the old to live in peace and comfort...

礼之用，和为贵〔106〕

In conducting the rites, seeking harmony is the most valuable principle.

里仁为美〔108〕

One should choose to dwell in such a place where there are men of benevolence.

M

名不正，则言不顺〔110〕

If names are not rectified, what is said will not sound reasonable.

Q

其身正，不令而行〔112〕

If the ruler acts properly, the common people will obey him without being ordered to.

巧言令色〔114〕

A man who speaks with honeyed words and pretends to be kind cannot be benevolent.

巧言乱德〔116〕

Sweet words will ruin one's virtue.

群居终日，言不及义〔118〕

Those who spend the whole day long merely chatting idly...

R

人而无信，不知其可也〔120〕

How can one be acceptable without being trustworthy in words?

人莫不饮食也〔122〕

Everyone drinks and eats...

人无远虑，必有近忧〔124〕

Worries will soon appear if one gives no thought to a

long-term plan.

人一能之，己百之〔126〕

If others succeed by making one ounce of effort, I will make a hundred times as much effort.

仁者，人也，亲亲为大〔128〕

Being benevolent means to love people. The greatest benevolence is to love one's own parents.

S

三军可夺帅也〔130〕

An army may be deprived of its commanding officer...

三人行，必有我师焉〔132〕

When walking in the company of other men, there must be one I can learn something from.

士不可以不弘毅〔134〕

A scholar must be resolute and steadfast...

士见危致命，见得思义〔136〕

It is satisfactory for a gentleman to lay down his life...

逝者如斯夫，不舍昼夜〔138〕

"Time is going on like this river, flowing away endlessly day and night."

岁寒，然后知松柏之后凋也〔140〕

Only when the weather turns cold can we see that the leaves of pines and cypresses are the last to wither and fall.

W

为政以德〔142〕

He who rules his state on a moral basis would be supported by the people...

温故而知新〔144〕

If one is able to acquire new knowledge by reviewing old knowledge...

我非生而知之者〔146〕

I was not born with knowledge...

吾日三省吾身〔148〕

Every day I examine myself once and again...

吾十有五而志于学〔150〕

Since the age of fifteen, I have devoted myself to learning...

无欲速，无见小利〔152〕

Do not make haste; do not covet small gains.

X

小不忍，则乱大谋〔154〕

Lack of patience in small matters will bring destruction to overall plans.

性相近也，习相远也〔156〕

Men are similar to one another by nature. They diverge gradually as a result of different customs.

学而不思则罔〔158〕

It throws one into bewilderment to read without thinking. . .

学而不厌，悔人不倦〔160〕

Study hard and never feel contented, and never be tired of teaching others.

学而时习之，不亦说乎〔162〕

"Is it not a pleasure after all to practice in due time what one has learnt?

Y

言顾行，行顾言〔164〕

When a man speaks, he should think of his acts; when he acts, he should think of what he said.

一张一弛，文武之道也〔166〕

The principle of kings Wen and Wu was to alternate tension with relaxation.

益者三乐，损者三乐〔168〕

There are three kinds of beneficial pleasure. Equally there are three kinds of harmful pleasure.

益者三友，损者三友〔170〕

Confucius said, "There are three kinds of people one may make friends with. Equally, there are three kinds of people one should not make friends with."

有德者必有言〔172〕

A virtuous man must have said something of note.

有教无类〔174〕

In educating people, I treat everyone the same.

愚而好自用〔176〕

A foolish man likes to think himself clever...

Z

朝闻道，夕死可矣〔178〕

If one learns the truth in the morning, one would never regret dying the same evening.

知之为知之，不知为不知〔180〕

If you understand what you learn，say you do；if not，say you do not.

知之者不如好之者〔182〕

To be fond of knowledge is better than merely to acquire it.

知者不惑，仁者不忧〔184〕

A wise man is never cheated，a virtuous man is never worried. . .

知者不失人，亦不失言〔186〕

A wise man shall not let a man slip into uselessness，nor shall he waste his words.

知者乐水，仁者乐山〔188〕

The wise take delight in water，the benevolent in mountains.

志士仁人，无求生以害仁〔190〕

A man of benevolence and lofty ideals should not，at the expense of benevolence，cling cravenly to life instead of braving death.

志于道，据于德〔192〕

Stick to the way to your goal，base yourself on virtue.

质胜文则野，文胜质则史〔194〕

One would seem uncouth with more simplicity than refinement, and seem superficial with more refinement than simplicity.

中人以上，可以语上也〔196〕

Advanced knowledge can be transmitted to those who are above the average. . .

主忠信，无友不如己者〔198〕

A gentleman should pay great attention to loyalty and sincerity, and not make close friends with those whose morality is inferior to his.

自古皆有死，民无信不立〔200〕

Man has been destined to die since time immemorial. But if people lose their trust in the government then the country has lost its basis.

孔子说

CONFUCIUS SAYS

孔子，姓孔名丘，字仲尼。春秋末鲁国人。先世为宋国贵族，殷王室后裔。孔子六世祖孔父嘉（字孔父，名嘉）曾任宋大司马，后被杀，依周制，其后代以孔为氏，避宋乱奔鲁，孔家由大夫降为士。

公元前551年（鲁襄公二十二年）孔子出生在曲阜尼丘山一个山洞里，因其"生而首上圩顶，故因名曰丘字仲尼"。孔子在鲁国长期聚徒讲学，开私人讲学的风气，传说弟子三千，身通六艺者七十二人，创立儒家学派。孔子曾任鲁大司寇，后辞官带弟子周游列国，晚年回到鲁国一边讲学，一边著书立说。

孔子贵仁，其名言曰："克己复礼为仁。一日克己复礼，天下归仁焉。""仁者不忧，知者不惑，勇者不惧。""己所不欲，勿施于人。"

Confucius' name was Kong Qiu with the courtesy name Zhongni. He was a native of the State of Lu at late Spring and Autumn Period. His ancestor was noble in the State of Song and descendant of the royal Yin family of the Shang Dynasty. His sixth ancestor'Kongfu Jia used to be the Minister of Defense of the State of Song, and later was killed. According to Zhou system, his descendants took Kong as the family name. Later to escape the chaos in the State of Song, they fled to the State of Lu, and the Kong family was degraded to Shi (social stratum between senior officials and the common people) from Dafu (senior official).

In 551 BC (the 22nd year under the reign of Lu Xianggong), Confucius was born in a cave on the Niqiu Mountain in Qufu. "Born a concave head whose shape resembled the hill Qiu, he was named Qiu and styled Zhongni." Confucius gathered people and gave speeches in the State of Lu, starting the trend of private teaching. It is said that he had 3,000 students, 72 of whom were well versed in the six classical arts—rites, music, archery, riding, writing and arithmetic. And thus he established the school of Confucianism. Confucius once held the post of the Minister of Justice in the State of Lu, and later he resigned and toured the states with his students. In his old days, he returned to the State of Lu, giving lectures while writing books to expound his doctrines. Confucius valued humaneness. His famous dictums include: "To completely overcome selfishness and keep to propriety is humaneness. If for a full day the ruler can overcome selfishness and keep to propriety, everyone in the world will return to humaneness." "The wise are not confused, the humane are not anxious, the brave are not afraid." "Do not impose upon others what you do not desire yourself."

爱之，能勿劳乎

To love him means not to let him indulge in comfort. . .

爱之，能勿劳乎？忠焉，能勿诲乎？

《论语·宪问》

Confucius said,“To love him means not to let him indulge in comfort;to be loyal to him means to teach him.”

【注释】

爱之，能勿劳乎：爱子，故曰“爱之”，“劳”，是为父之道。《战国策·赵策》：“父母之爱子，则为之计深远。”故要“劳之”，不能让他贪图安逸。《左传·隐公三年》：“爱子，教之以义方，弗纳于邪。”**忠**：忠诚。《论语·学而》：“为人谋而不忠乎？”

【译文】

孔子说：“爱他，就不能让他贪图安逸。忠于他，就不能不对他进行教诲。”

饱食终日，无所用心

He who always has a full stomach but does nothing meaningful is simply a good-for-nothing.

饱食终日，无所用心，难矣哉！

《论语·阳货》

He who always has a full stomach but does nothing meaningful is simply a good-for-nothing.

【注释】

饱食终日，无所用心：孔子主张“君子食无求饱，居无求安”（《论语·学而》）、“饭疏食饮水，曲肱而枕之，乐亦在其中矣”（《论语·述而》）。所以，他特别讨厌那些“饱食终日，无所用心”的人，认为这些人不会有什么出息。

【译文】

孔子说：“整天吃饱饭没事干的人，不会有什么出息。”

博学于文，约之以礼

A gentleman will not go astray...

君子广泛地学习文化典籍，并用礼来约束自己，就可避免离经叛道了。

博学于文，约之以礼，亦可以弗畔矣夫！

《论语·颜渊》

A gentleman will not go astray so long as he studies extensively and regulates himself with the rites.

【注释】

博学：学问广博。《墨子·非儒下》：“博学不可使议世。”**约**：约束。**畔**：违背，背叛，通“叛”。**矣夫**：同“矣”，兼表推测。

【译文】

孔子说：“君子广泛地学习文化典籍，并用礼来约束自己，就可避免离经叛道了。”

不愤不启，不悱不发

I will not enlighten my students until they have really tried hard. . .

不愤不启，不悱不发。

《论语·述而》

I will not enlighten my students until they have really tried hard but failed to understand. I will not instruct them until they have something to say but fail to make themselves understood.

【注释】

愤（fèn）：憋闷，郁积，怎么想也想不明白。**悱**（fěi）：心里想说又说不出来。**发**：启发。“不启”、“不发”是孔子的教学方法。

【译文】

孔子说：“我教学生的方法是：不到他们苦思冥想也不能明白的时候，不去开导他们；不到他们心里想说又总说不明白的时候，不去启发他们。”

不患人之不己知

Do not worry that your abilities are not appreciated...

不患人之不己知，患其不能也。

《论语·宪问》

Do not worry that your abilities are not appreciated. Just make sure that you possess them.

【注释】

相类的话在《论语》里出现过四次：《学而》："子曰：'不患人之不己知，患不知人也。'"《里仁》："子曰：'不患莫己知，求为可知也。'"《卫灵公》："子曰：'君子病无能焉，不病人之不己知也。'"加上这段话共四次，故朱熹注曰：孔子"于此一事，盖屡言之，其丁宁之意亦可见矣。"（《论语集注》）王夫之注曰："能夺我名而不能夺我志，能困我于境遇而不能困我于天人无愧之中，不患也。"（《四书训义》）

【译文】

孔子说："不怕别人不了解自己，就怕自己没有真才实学。"

不患无位，患所以立

Don't worry about having no official position, but do worry about your ability to fulfill a post.

不患无位，患所以立。

《论语·里仁》

Don't worry about having no official position, but do worry about your ability to fulfill a post.

【注释】

不患无位，患所以立： 患，担心。立，站立，引伸为任职。孔子认为只要自己具有任职的本领，是否能得到职位那是机遇问题，而机遇往往是不可求的。

【译文】

孔子说："不愁没有职位，只愁没有任职的本领。"

不义而富且贵，于我如浮云

Ill-gotten wealth and rank are just like fleeting clouds to me.

用不正当的手段得来的富贵，对我来说就像浮云一样。

不义而富且贵，于我如浮云。

《论语·述而》

Ill-gotten wealth and rank are just like fleeting clouds to me.

【注释】

朱熹《论语集注》：“其视不义之富贵，如浮云之无有，漠然无所动于其中也。”孔子反对以不义的手段取得财富与官位。虽然他说过：“富与贵，是人之所欲也”（《论语·里仁》），但他更主张君子对富贵要“取之有道”。

【译文】

孔子说：“用不正当的手段得来的富贵，对我来说就像浮云一样。”

不在其位，不谋其政

Do not get involved in the government affairs that are not your responsibility.

不在其位，不谋其政。

《论语·宪问》

Do not get involved in the government affairs that are not your responsibility.

【注释】

不在其位，不谋其政：同样的话在《论语·泰伯》里出现过。清·刘宝楠《论语正义》："欲各专一于其职。"这也是儒家一贯的处世态度。后世孟子也说过"位卑而言高，罪也"的话。"君子素其位而行，不愿乎其外"。(《中庸》)

【译文】

孔子说："不在那个职位，就不谋划那方面的政事。"

大德不逾闲

As long as one does not step out of bounds in big matters...

大德不逾闲，小德出入可也。

《论语·子张》

Zi Xia said, "As long as one does not step out of bounds in big matters, it is permissible for one not to be meticulous."

【注释】

大德、小德：一般解释为大节，小节。朱熹《论语集注》："大德、小德，犹言大节、小节。人能先立乎其大者，则小节虽或未尽合理，亦无害也。"**逾**：就是超越。**闲**：原指栅栏，指界限。孔子主张用人之道看其大节，而不求全责备。《论语·微子》篇中周公语曰："无求备于一人。"宋·苏轼说过："用人不求其备，嘉善而矜不能。"《汉书·陈汤传》："论大功者不录小过，举大善者不庇细瑕。"甚至后世儒家主张"掩其小故以全大德"。(宋·欧阳修《文正范公神道碑铭序》)

【译文】

子夏说："人在大节上不能超越界限，在小节上有些出入是应当允许的。"

当仁，不让于师

In the face of benevolence, do not give precedence even to your teacher.

当仁，不让于师。

《论语·卫灵公》

In the face of benevolence, do not give precedence even to your teacher.

【注释】

当仁：“当仁”有两种解释：一为面临仁德；一为担当实现仁道之重任。朱熹注：“当仁，以仁为己任也。虽师亦无所逊，言当勇往而必为也。盖仁者，人所自有而自为之，非有争也，何逊之有?”（《论语集注》）**师**：一般解释为“师长”，也有人解释为“众人”。

【译文】

孔子说：“面临仁德时，不必让老师先行。”

道不同，不相为谋

People who follow different political paths do not take counsel with one another.

道不同，不相为谋。

《论语·卫灵公》

People who follow different political paths do not take counsel with one another.

【注释】

道不同，不相为谋：道，指一定的人生观、世界观、政治主张或思想体系。但不同学派赋予道的含义不同。孔子这里讲的是一条结交的原则。以道同为原则，道不同，不相为谋。因为彼此政治主张不同，就无法互相探讨。交友也是一样，不同道的人难以相友。因为“友者，所以相有也；道不同，何以相友也”。（《荀子·大略》）

【译文】

孔子说：“政治主张不同，不互相探讨谋划。”

道之以政，齐之以刑

Regulated by the edicts and punishments. . .

道之以政，齐之以刑，民免而无耻；道之以德，齐之以礼，有耻且格。

《论语·为政》

Regulated by the edicts and punishments, people will know only how to stay out of trouble but will not have a sense of shame. Guided by virtues and the rites, they will not only have a sense of shame but also know how to correct their mistakes of their own accord.

【注释】

道：本意是道路，在《论语》里多次出现，多引申为政治路线或政治主张。“礼之用，和为贵，先王之道，斯为美。”（《论语·学而》）“夫子之道，忠恕而已矣。”（《论语·里仁》）**齐**：整治。**免**：逃避，避免。**格**：纠正。

【译文】

孔子说：“靠行政命令和刑罚来制约人民，老百姓只知避免犯罪遭刑罚而不会有廉耻之心；如果用道德和礼教来引导人民，老百姓不仅知道犯罪是耻辱的事情，而且能自己改正错误。”

德不孤，必有邻

A man of virtue can never be isolated. He is sure to have like-minded companions.

德不孤，必有邻。

《论语·里仁》

A man of virtue can never be isolated. He is sure to have like-minded companions.

【注释】

德不孤，必有邻：朱熹认为："德不孤是同声相应，同气相求，吉人为善，便自有志人相伴。"《大戴礼记·曾子立事》："君子义则有常，善则有邻。"

【译文】

孔子说："有道德的人是不会孤立的，一定会有志同道合者相从。"

弟子，入则孝，出则悌

At home, a young man should be dutiful towards his parents...

弟子，入则孝，出则悌，谨而信，泛爱众而亲仁。

《论语·学而》

At home, a young man should be dutiful towards his parents; going outside, he should be respectful towards his elders; he should be cautious in deeds and trustworthy in words; he should love everyone yet make close friends only with those of benevolence.

【注释】

谨：寡言。**泛爱众：**博爱众人。孔子的泛爱众不同于墨家的“兼爱”，是爱自己的亲人然后推及他人。孔子认为“泛爱众”只是“亲仁”而不是仁的全部。**亲仁：**亲近有仁德的人。

【译文】

孔子说：“少年在家里孝顺父母，敬爱兄长，做事谨慎认真，说话诚实，博爱大众而亲近有仁德的人。”

发愤忘食，乐以忘忧

The Duke of Ye asked Zi Lu about Confucius. . .

发愤忘食，乐以忘忧，不知老之将至云尔。

《论语·述而》

The Duke of Ye asked Zi Lu about Confucius, Zi Lu failed to give a reply. Confucius said to him afterwards, "Why did you not say something like this: He is the sort of person who can be so diligent that he forgets his meals, so happy that he forgets his worries and is even unaware of approaching old age.

【注释】

云尔：云，如此；尔，同"耳"，而已，罢了。近人康有为《论语注》："忘食，则不知贫贱；忘忧，则不知苦戚；忘老，则不知死生；非至人安能至此。"

【译文】

（叶公向子路问孔子的为人，子路不知如何回答）孔子对子路说："你为什么不这样说：他的为人，发愤用功便忘记吃饭，快乐便忘记忧愁，不晓得衰老会要到来，如此而已。"

父母在，不远游

When one's parents are alive, one should not go far away.

父母在，不远游，游必有方。

《论语·里仁》

When one's parents are alive, one should not go far away. If one has to, one should tell them where one is going.

【注释】

父母在，不远游： 孔子讲“父母在，不远游”是从“孝亲”的角度来说的，父母在堂，儿子远出，就不能侍奉父母了。但并不是说父母在堂就绝对不能出远门，孔子只是强调“游必有方”，就是说一定让父母知道你的去处。

【译文】

孔子说：“父母在堂，不出远门，如必须外出，一定要让父母知道去处。”

父母之年，不可不知也

One must always keep in mind one's parents' birthdays. . .

父母之年，不可不知也。一则以喜，一则以惧。

《论语·里仁》

One must always keep in mind one's parents' birthdays. On the one hand, one is glad to offer birthday congratulations; on the other, one is worried to see they grow one year older.

【注释】

父母之年，不可不知也：孔子最重孝悌，他认为孝悌是仁的基础，“孝子之至，莫大于尊亲”。他认为对父母的尊敬亲爱，不仅限于对父母的赡养，而且应该时时心存孝敬之情，故说：“父母之年，不可不知也。”

【译文】

孔子说：“父母的年龄（生日）不能不时时记到心里。一方面为他们长寿而高兴，另一方面为他们又老一岁而忧虑。”

富而可求也

I would pursue wealth so long as it could be obtained legitimately.

财富如果来路正当，就是替人执鞭的下等差役我也可以干。

富而可求也，虽执鞭之士，吾亦为之。

《论语·述而》

I would pursue wealth so long as it could be obtained legitimately, even by being a common cart driver.

【注释】

执鞭之士：根据《周礼》，执鞭之士可能指两种人，一种是天子或诸侯出行时，有二至八人执鞭清道，让闲杂人回避。一种是古代市场的守门人，执鞭维持秩序。鄙以为孔子所指应该包括为人赶车的下等差役。当孔子听到达巷党人说他虽博学却无一专长时，他对弟子们说："我干什么好呢？赶车？做射手？我替人赶车好了。"他还说过："吾少也贱，故多能鄙事。"（《论语·子罕》）

【译文】

孔子说："财富如果来路正当，就是替人执鞭的下等差役我也可以干。"

富与贵，是人之所欲也

Everyone desires money and high position...

富与贵，是人之所欲也；不以其道得之，不处也。贫与贱，是人之所恶也；不以其道得之，不去也。

《论语·里仁》

Everyone desires money and high position, but a gentleman would not accept them unless he got them in a right way. Everyone hates poverty and low status, but a gentleman would not get rid of them in an unjust way.

【注释】

得之：“富与贵”，是人人都想得到的，故说“得之”；“贫与贱”，却不是人人都想得到的，也说“得之”。前“得之”意为“得到”；后“得之”意为“去之”。

【译文】

孔子说：“金钱和地位，这是人人都想得到的，但君子不会用不正当的方法得到它。贫穷和下贱，这是人人都厌恶的，但君子不会用不正当的方法摆脱它。”

工欲善其事，必先利其器

A craftsman must prepare his tools beforehand in order to do his work well.

工匠要想做好他的工作，一定要先准备好他的工具。

工欲善其事，必先利其器。

《论语·卫灵公》

A craftsman must prepare his tools beforehand in order to do his work well.

【注释】

工欲善其事，必先利其器：善：做好。**利：**精良。器，工具。工匠要想做好他的工作，一定要先使工具精良。孔子是以利器喻为仁。

【译文】

孔子说:“工匠要想做好他的工作，一定要先准备好他的工具。”

躬自厚而薄责于人

Being strict with oneself and lenient to others is sure to save one from ill will.

躬自厚而薄责于人，则远怨矣。

《论语·卫灵公》

Being strict with oneself and lenient to others is sure to save one from ill will.

【注释】

躬自厚而薄责于人：西汉董仲舒解释说："以仁治人，义治我，躬自厚而薄责于人，此之谓也。""责己厚，故身益修；责人薄，故人易从，所以人不得而怨之。"（朱熹《论语集注》）

【译文】

孔子说："多自责而少责备人，自然就可以避免怨恨了。"

古之言之不出

In ancient times, people didn't say things lightly...

古者言之不出，耻躬之不逮也。

《论语·里仁》

In ancient times, people didn't say things lightly, as they would be ashamed not to be able to match up to their words.

【注释】

耻：动词主动用法，以为可耻的意思，**逮**（dài）：及，赶上。

【译文】

孔子说："古人不轻易说大话，因为怕自己说得出而做不到。"

过而不改，是谓过矣

Not to correct the mistake one has made is to err indeed.

过而不改，是谓过矣。

《论语·卫灵公》

Not to correct the mistake one has made is to err indeed.

【注释】

过而不改，是谓过矣：《韩诗外传》卷三引孔子的话说："过而改之，是不过也。"和这里的"过而不改，是谓过矣"正相解。《左传·宣公二年》："人谁无过，过而能改，善莫大焉。"人非圣贤，孰能无过。其实，即使圣贤，也难免犯错误。《论语·子张》篇中，子贡说："君子之过也，如日月之食焉。过也，人皆见之；更也，人皆仰之。"执政者的过错如日月之蚀，大家都看得到，当他改正了过错，大家更敬仰他。所以，孔子说"过则勿惮改"。（《论语·学而》）

【译文】

孔子说："有过错不改正，才是真错。"

过犹不及

Going too far and not going far enough are equally bad.

过犹不及

《论语·先进》

Going too far and not going far enough are equally bad.

【注释】

过犹不及：子贡问："颛孙师和卜商，哪个更好一些？"孔子说："颛孙师办事好过头，卜商办事好达不到。"子贡说："那么还是颛孙师好一些了？"孔子说："过犹不及。"意思是孔子认为"过头和达不到同样不好。"这是孔子哲学思想的方法论命题。意思是超过事物一定界限与未达到一定界限同样是错误的。孔子主张中庸，无过无不及。朱熹《论语集注》："道以中庸为至，贤智之过虽若胜于愚不肖之不及，然其失中则一也。""过犹不及"这个成语含有辩正法因素。

【译文】

孔子说："过头和达不到是一样的。"

好学近乎知

To be eager to learn indicates wisdom because it may eliminate stupidity.

好学近乎知，力行近乎仁，知耻近乎勇。

《中庸·问政章》

To be eager to learn indicates wisdom because it may eliminate stupidity. To practice what one knows indicates benevolence because it makes one selfless. To have a sense of shame indicates courage because it clears one of cowardice.

【注释】

知、仁、勇：孔子说："知者不惑，仁者不忧，勇者不惧。"（《论语·子罕》）"知、仁、勇三者，天下之达德也。"（《礼记·中庸》）

【译文】

孔子说："好学足以破愚所以接近于智慧，身体力行足以忘私所以接近于仁爱，知耻足以起懦所以接近于勇敢。"

后生可畏

Young people have great potential for achievements.

后生可畏，焉知来者之不如今也？

《论语·子罕》

Young people have great potential for achievements. Who can say that they will not be our equals in the future?

【注释】

后生：指后辈。**畏**：敬畏。反映了孔子对青年人的期望与爱护。荀子说过“青，取之于蓝而青于蓝”的话与此义相近。孔子这句话后还说：“如果一个人到了四五十岁还没有什么名望的话，也就不会有什么作为了。”这可看作是孔子激励弟子“及时自勉”的话。

【译文】

孔子说：“年轻人是大有作为的，谁能断定他们将来不如我们这一代呢？”

己所不欲，勿施于人

Do not impose upon others what you do not desire yourself.

己所不欲，勿施于人。

《论语·卫灵公》

Do not impose upon others what you do not desire yourself.

【注释】

己所不欲，勿施于人：在《论语》里这句话出现两次，一次是仲弓（冉雍）问仁，孔子说了这句话。一次是孔子对子贡说恕，孔子常以恕释仁。朱熹注："恕，推己以及人也。"（《论语集注》）

【译文】

孔子说："自己不想做的事情，就不要加给别人。"

见善如不及，见不善如探汤

Striving to be the first and fearing to lag behind...

见善如不及，见不善如探汤。

《论语·季氏》

Striving to be the first and fearing to lag behind when seeking goodness; retreating as quickly as if hurt by boiling water when avoiding vices.

【注释】

见善如不及，见不善如探汤：探汤，探沸水则把手烫伤。比喻戒惧之意。孔子的意思是让人积善去恶。做善人，听善言，行善政。

【译文】

孔子说："追求善良，要争先恐后；避开邪恶，要像开水烫手一样急迫。"

见贤思齐焉

When you meet a man of virtue, learn from him.

见贤思齐焉，见不贤而内自省也。

《论语·里仁》

When you meet a man of virtue, learn from him. When you meet a man without virtue, examine yourself to see if you have the same defects as he has.

【注释】

贤：贤人，儒家指德才兼备的人。孔子提倡向贤人学习，多结交贤人。还主张“举贤才”。**自省**：亦称内省。儒家提倡的一种修养方法。意即自我反省，孔子弟子曾参曾说：“吾日三省吾身。”

【译文】

孔子说：“遇见才德好的人，就应该向他看齐，遇到无德才的人，就应反省自己有没有和他同样的毛病。”

敬鬼神而远之

If one respects the spirits of the dead and the gods...

敬鬼神而远之，可谓知矣。

《论语·雍也》

If one respects the spirits of the dead and the gods while keeping them at a distance, then he can be called wise.

【注释】

敬鬼神而远之：这是孔子对待鬼神的态度。孔子在其承认有鬼神的前提下，又提出对鬼神敬而远之（既不轻慢又不亲近）的态度。孔子主张重人事而轻鬼神。“未能事人，焉能事鬼?”（论语·先进）朱熹《论语集注》曰：“专用力于人道之所宜，而不惑于鬼神之不可知，知者之事也。”

【译文】

孔子说:“对鬼神采取敬而远之的态度，可以算是聪明了。”

君子不器

A gentleman should not be like a utensil.

君子不器。

《论语 · 为政》

A gentleman should not be like a utensil. (He should have broad knowledge and not be confined to one use.)

【注释】

君子不器：器，本指容器。容器因有专用而呈不同的形状。后指人的才能、本领（特指专长）。《礼记 · 王制》：“暗聋、跛躄、断者、侏儒、百工、各以其器食之。”意思是，这些人各依靠自己的一技之长而生活。古代知识范围比较狭窄，各行有各行的知识范围，懂得一行的知识，就可以立世吃饭。孔子认为君子应该无所不通。后人还说“一事之不知，儒者之耻。”虽然当时有人批评孔子“博学而无所成名”，（《论语 · 子罕》）但孔子仍主张“君子不器”。

【译文】

孔子说：“君子应有广博的知识。”

君子不以言举人

A gentleman does not promote a man whose words are pleasant to his ear.

君子不以言举人，不以人废言。

《论语·卫灵公》

A gentleman does not promote a man whose words are pleasant to his ear, neither does he disdain his correct words for he is an unpleasant man.

【注释】

孔子认为对一个人的认识不能只听他如何说，重要的是看他怎样做。不仅听他的言论，更要看他的行动。《史记·孙子吴起传》："能行之者未必能言，能言之者未必能行。"在中国历史上，"以言举人"而废事的例子很多，战国时赵将赵括和三国时蜀将马谡都是"能言"却不"能行"的典型。"以人废言"的例子就更多了。曾国藩"其人不可取"，但其确实讲过、写过不少至理名言。"以言举人"不好，"以人废言"也不好。

【译文】

孔子说："执政者不因人说好听的话就提拔他们，也不因他是坏人就鄙弃他说过的正确的话。"

君子耻其言而过其行

A gentleman takes it as a disgrace to let his words outstrip his deeds.

君子耻其言而过其行。

《论语·宪问》

A gentleman takes it as a disgrace to let his words outstrip his deeds.

【注释】

君子耻其言而过其行： 孔子注重言行一致，更强调行。他说过“君子以行言，小人以舌言”。(《孔子家语·颜回》) 在《论语》里有“敏于事而慎于言”。(《论语·学而》)“君子欲讷于言而敏于行”。(《论语·里仁》)“听其言而观其行”(《论语·公冶长》) 等语义相同的话，可见孔子对言与行的态度。

【译文】

孔子说:“君子以说得多，做得少为耻辱。”

君子成人之美

A gentleman helps others fulfill good deeds...

君子成人之美，不成人之恶。

《论语·颜渊》

A gentleman helps others fulfill good deeds and never helps them in bad deeds.

【注释】

君子成人之美：朱熹《论语集注》："成者，诱掖奖劝以成其事也。"《大戴礼记·曾子立事》："君子己善，亦乐人之善也。己能，亦乐人之能也。"与孔子语意相近。

【译文】

孔子说："君子成全别人的好事，不去促成别人的坏事。"

君子固穷

When gentlemen become impoverished, they can still persevere in virtue.

君子固穷，小人穷斯滥矣。

《论语·卫灵公》

When gentlemen become impoverished, they can still persevere in virtue; when petty men are impoverished, they will act in defiance of virtue.

【注释】

君子固穷，小人穷斯滥矣：孔子周游列国时在陈国断绝了粮食，跟随他的人都饿病了，不能起床。子路来见孔子埋怨说："君子也有穷困的时候吗?"孔子说了这句话。他认为，君子不会因为穷困而改变操守，人小往往经受不住穷困的考验，一遇穷困就会胡作非为。

【译文】

孔子说："君子虽遇穷困，但能坚持，小人一遇穷困便胡作非为了。"

君子和而不同

A gentleman unites with people of principle and never follows others blindly.

君子和而不同，小人同而不和。

《论语·子路》

A gentleman unites with people of principle and never follows others blindly. A petty man follows others blindly without regard to principle.

【注释】

和、同：都是孔子哲学思想的范畴，“和”指不同事物之间的协调、统一、平衡，孔子主张以其仁、礼统一的学说作为协和各种意见的基本准则。“同”指事物的绝对等同。朱熹注：“和者无乖戾之心，同者有阿比之意。”（《论语集注》）

【译文】

孔子说：“君子讲有原则的团结而不盲从附和，小人只是盲从附和而不讲原则。”

君子谋道不谋食

A gentleman devotes himself to studying the academic system of ideology instead of seeking food and clothing.

君子谋道不谋食

《论语 · 卫灵公》

A gentleman devotes himself to studying the academic system of ideology instead of seeking food and clothing.

【注释】

谋道不谋食：孔子的政治与经济思想。孔子主张士人应以弘道为志，所谋求的是道的实行，故不必亲自耕织，谋求衣食。他说过："耕也，馁在其中矣；学也，禄在其中矣。"（《论语 · 卫灵公》）

【译文】

孔子说："君子用心力于学术思想体系的研究，不用心力于谋求衣食。"

君子求诸己，小人求诸人

A gentleman sets strict demands on himself while a petty man sets strict demands on others.

君子求诸己，小人求诸人。

《论语·卫灵公》

A gentleman sets strict demands on himself while a petty man sets strict demands on others.

【注释】

君子求诸己，小人求诸人： 求，责也。儒家把“反求诸己”作为区别君子和小人的标准。《礼记·中庸》曰：“射有以乎君子，失诸正鹄，反求诸其身。”

【译文】

孔子说：“君子严格要求自己，小人苛刻要求别人。”

君子去仁，恶乎成名

How can one be called a gentleman if one betrays benevolence.

君子去仁，恶乎成名？君子无终食之间违仁，造次必于是，颠沛必于是。

《论语·里仁》

How can one be called a gentleman if one betrays benevolence? Under no circumstances should a gentleman forget to practice benevolence.

【注释】

去：离开。**恶**（wū）：何处。**违**：离开。**造次**：仓促，急遽。**颠沛**：倾覆，仆倒。用以形容人事困顿，社会动乱。

【译文】

孔子说："君子离开了仁德还怎么称得上君子呢？君子在任何情况下都不会忘记实行仁德。"

君子食无求饱，居无求安

A gentleman seeks neither a full belly nor a comfortable home.

君子吃饭不求饱足,居住不求舒适,办事敏捷,说话谨慎,向得道之人学习以改正自己的缺点,这样就可以说是好学了。

君子食无求饱，居无求安，敏于事而慎于言，就有道而正焉，可谓好学也已。

《论语·学而》

A gentleman seeks neither a full belly nor a comfortable home. Instead, he is quick in action yet cautious in speech. He learns from virtuous and accomplished men in order to correct his mistakes. Such can be called a man with eagerness to study.

【注释】

君子：《论语》中的“君子”有时指执政者，有时指“有德之人”。**正**：纠正，匡正。

【译文】

孔子说：“君子吃饭不求饱足，居住不求舒适，办事敏捷，说话谨慎，向得道之人学习以改正自己的缺点，这样就可以说是好学了。”

君子坦荡荡，小人长戚戚

A gentleman is always broad-minded while a petty man is always full of anxiety.

君子坦荡荡，小人长戚戚。

《论语·述而》

A gentleman is always broad-minded while a petty man is always full of anxiety.

【注释】

坦荡荡：坦，安也。荡荡，广远貌。君子通达事理，故待人接物犹如行走在平坦大道上，安祥而舒泰。**长戚戚**：戚戚，忧虑貌。小人心思常为物役，患得患失，故常怀戚戚之心。

【译文】

孔子说："君子心胸坦荡，小人忧心忡忡。"

君子泰而不骄

A gentleman always keeps even-tempered without being arrogant...

君子泰而不骄，小人骄而不泰。

《论语·子路》

A gentleman always keeps even-tempered without being arrogant while a petty man is arrogant without being even-tempered.

【注释】

泰而不骄：是孔子提出君子治政应有的五种美德之一。孔子主张君子对人，无论其人数多少，势力大小，都不应有所怠慢，那样君子居其位就能安详舒泰而不致傲慢无礼。**骄而不泰**：孔子指一种待人处事的傲慢矜夸态度。骄与不骄，泰与不泰，不仅作为君子小人的区别，而且也带来了他们安泰与否的不同境遇。

【译文】

孔子说："君子心情平和而不傲慢，小人傲慢而心情不平和。"

君子以文会友

"A gentleman makes friends through his learning. . . "

君子以文会友，以友辅仁。

《论语·颜渊》

Zeng Zi said, "A gentleman makes friends through his learning and cultivates virtue and benevolence through those friends."

【注释】

这是孔子弟子曾参说的话。曾参，字子舆，春秋末鲁国人，少孔子四十六岁。其父曾点，也受业于孔子。曾参性内向，处事谨慎，看似迟钝。孔子说“参也鲁”。(《论语·先进》) 但他深谙孔子仁道之内涵，认为“夫子之道，忠恕而已”。(《论语·里仁》) 以“孝”著称。重视修身，提出“吾日三省吾身”。(《论语·学而》) 孔子死后，授徒讲学影响深远，相传他为思、孟学派的鼻祖，在孔子以后的儒经传授上有重要地位，被尊称“曾子”。

【译文】

曾子说:“君子用文章学问聚会朋友，藉朋友帮助培养仁德。”

君子忧道不忧贫

What a gentleman worries about is not poverty but if there are right principles throughout the country.

君子忧道不忧贫。

《论语·卫灵公》

What a gentleman worries about is not poverty but if there are right principles throughout the country.

【注释】

忧道不忧贫：孔子的政治愿望是“天下有道”（《论语·季氏》），而以天下无道为忧虑。他主张“学以致其道”（《论语·子张》），而不应为物质生活的贫困忧虑。孔子“忧道不忧贫”的思想，对后世儒家影响很大。

【译文】

孔子说：“君子忧虑的是天下有道无道，而不是物质生活的贫穷。”

君子有九思

A gentleman concentrates on the following nine things...

君子有九思：视思明，听思聪，色思温，貌思恭，言思忠，事思敬，疑思问，忿思难，见得思义。

《论语·季氏》

A gentleman concentrates on the following nine things: seeing clearly when he uses his eyes; hearing acutely when he uses his ears; looking mild when it comes to facial expression; appearing sedate when it comes to demeanour; being sincere when he speaks; being conscientious when it comes to his office responsibility; seeking advice when he is in the face of difficulty; foreseeing the consequences when he gets angry; asking himself whether it is right when he wants to gain something.

【注释】

九思：在《论语》里孔子强调“思”的几种情况：一是强调思和行的关系。“季文子三思而后行”（《论语·公冶长》）；二是强调思和学的关系。“学而不思则罔，思而不学则殆”（《论语·为政》）；三是强调思和感知的关系。如本章。

【译文】

孔子说:“君子要考虑九件事：看的时候，要考虑是否看明白了。听的时候，要考虑是否听清楚了。脸上的颜色，要考虑是否温和。容貌态度，要考虑是否端庄。与人交谈，要考虑是否诚恳。对待工作，要考虑是否认真负责。遇到疑难，要考虑如何向人请教。将要发怒时，要考虑会有什么后患。要得到什么，先要考虑是否应该得到。”

君子有三戒

A gentleman should maintain vigilance against three things. . .

君子有三戒：少之时，血气未定，戒之在色；及其壮也，血气方刚，戒之在斗；及其老也，血气既衰，戒之在得。

《论语·季氏》

A gentleman should maintain vigilance against three things: In youth when the vital spirits are not yet settled, he should be on guard against lusting for feminine beauty; in the prime of life when the vital spirits are exuberant, he should be on guard against being bellicose; in old age when the vital spirits are on the decline, he should be on guard against insatiable avarice.

【注释】

三戒：儒家道德修养的内容。指戒色、戒斗、戒得。《淮南子·诠言训》："凡人之性，少则猖狂，壮则暴强，老则好利。"意本于孔子之言。

【译文】

孔子说："君子有三件事要警惕：年少时，血气还没有稳定，要警惕贪恋女色；到了壮年，血气正旺盛，要警惕争强好斗；到了老年，血气已经衰竭，要警惕贪得无厌。"

君子欲讷于言而敏于行

A gentleman should be careful in speech and quick to act.

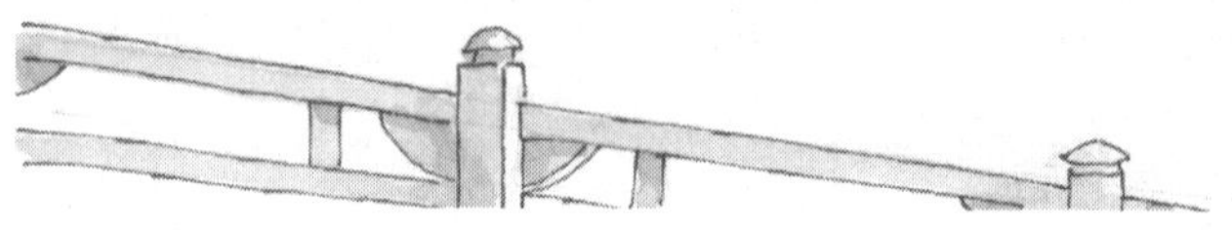

君子欲讷于言而敏于行。

《论语·里仁》

A gentleman should be careful in speech and quick to act.

【注释】

讷（nà）：言语迟钝。**讷于言而敏于行**：在《学而》篇中孔子说："敏于事而慎于言"，意思相近。

【译文】

孔子说："君子应该说话谨慎，做事勤劳敏捷。"

君子之过也，如日月之食焉

The gentleman's errors are like an eclipse of the sun and the moon. . .

君子之过也，如日月之食焉。过也，人皆见之；更也，人皆仰之。

《论语·子张》

Zi Gong said, "The gentleman's errors are like an eclipse of the sun and the moon: the whole world will see it when he errs, and he will be respected by all when he mends his ways."

【注释】

这是孔子弟子子贡说的话。**子贡**：姓端木，名赐，字子贡。春秋末卫国人。少孔子三十一岁。在孔门弟子中，善经商，家富有。利口巧辞，善于外交。思路敏捷，理解力强。相传其“事孔子一年，自谓过孔子；二年，自谓与孔子同；三年，自知不及孔子。”（《论衡·讲瑞》）后极力维护孔子的尊崇地位。**食**：同“蚀”。**仰**：敬仰。

【译文】

子贡说：“执政者的过错，好比日蚀月蚀一样挂在天上，对他的过错，人人都看得见；改正之后，大家更敬仰他。”

君子贞而不谅

A gentleman pays attention to faithfulness rather than small matters.

君子贞而不谅。

《论语·卫灵公》

A gentleman pays attention to faithfulness rather than small matters.

【注释】

贞：儒家伦理用词，意为正，遵循正道。朱熹《论语集注》："贞，正而固也。"孔子认为君子应坚持正道。**谅**：诚信，此处作固执，固守而不知变通解。孔子认为君子不应无原则地守信用。

【译文】

孔子说："君子重信义而不拘小节。"

苛政猛于虎

Tyranny is more cruel than a tiger.

苛税暴政之伤民甚于虎也。

苛政猛于虎。

《礼记·檀弓下》

Tyranny is more cruel than a tiger.

【注释】

鲁昭公二十五年（公元前517年），这一年孔子35岁。孔子决定和他的弟子们离开鲁国追随鲁君到齐国去。一天傍晚，孔子一行路过泰山脚下，看见一个妇人在墓侧哭得很伤心，就让子路上前去问。妇人说，她的公公、丈夫先后死于虎患，现在她的儿子又被老虎吃了。子路问她为什么不离开这里到平原去住，妇人回答说，这山里没有“苛政”。孔子听后感叹地说：“小子识之，苛政猛于虎也。”（《礼记·檀弓下》）喻苛税暴政之伤民甚于虎也。这件事反映了孔子的仁政和德治惠民的思想。

【译文】

孔子说：“苛税暴政之伤民甚于虎也。”

克己复礼为仁

One who restrains himself in order to observe the rites is benevolent.

克己复礼为仁。一日克己复礼，天下归仁焉。

《论语·颜渊》

(Yan Yuan asked what benevolence was.) Confucius said, "One who restrains himself in order to observe the rites is benevolent. Once you can do this, you will be unanimously considered a man of benevolence."

【注释】

克己复礼为仁："克己复礼"本是古代一成语。《左传·昭公十二年》："仲尼曰：'古也有志：克己复礼，仁也。'"可见在古代一种"志"书中早已有了这句话。孔子用前人的话赋予新的含义，强调实现它的条件和目的。**归仁**："称仁"的意思。

【译文】

（颜渊问老师什么是仁）孔子说："克制自己的言行合于礼就是仁。一旦能作到这样，人们就会承认你是仁人了。"

老者安之

I wish for the old to live in peace and comfort...

我愿老年人得到安逸,朋友们相互信任,少年人得到关怀。

老者安之，朋友信之，少者怀之。

《论语·公冶长》

I wish for the old to live in peace and comfort, friends to trust each other and the young to be taken good care of.

【注释】

老者安之，朋友信之，少者怀之：有一次颜渊、子路等在老师身边听讲。孔子说："说说你们自己的志向好吗?"子路说："我愿意把车马衣服同朋友共同使用，用坏了也决不抱怨。"颜渊说："我只想做到不夸耀自己的长处，不表白自己的功劳。"子路问孔子说："很想听听您的志向。"孔子说了上面的话。

【译文】

孔子说:"我愿老年人得到安逸，朋友们相互信任，少年人得到关怀。"

礼之用，和为贵

In conducting the rites, seeking harmony is the most valuable principle.

礼之用，和为贵。

《论语·学而》

In conducting the rites, seeking harmony is the most valuable principle.

【注释】

有子：有若（前518—?）孔子晚年弟子。姓有，名若，字子有。春秋末鲁国人。少孔子三十三岁。在孔门弟子中，特别重视“孝”与“礼”。提出“礼之用，和为贵”。孔子死后，门人以有若貌似孔子，曾一度被奉为师。在《论语》中独有若、曾子二人以字称，故有人认为《论语》实为有若和曾子之门人所编撰。**礼之用，和为贵：**儒家认为礼的社会功能在于调节人与人之间的关系，使之和谐。首先要用礼来调节统治者内部关系，“君使臣以礼，臣事君以忠”，其次用礼来教化庶民百姓，调节统治者和被统治者的关系。朱熹注曰：“和者，从容不迫之意。盖礼之为体虽严，然皆出于自然之理，故其为用，必从容而不迫，乃为可贵。先王之道，此其所以为美，而小事大事，无不由之也。”

【译文】

有子说：“礼的应用，以遇事和顺为可贵。”

里仁为美

One should choose to dwell in such a place where there are men of benevolence.

里仁为美，择不处仁，焉得知？

《论语·里仁》

One should choose to dwell in such a place where there are men of benevolence. Otherwise, how can one be said to be wise?

【注释】

里仁：指乡里中仁厚风俗。朱熹《论语集注》："里有仁厚之俗为美，择里而不居于是焉，则失其是非之本心，而不得为知矣。"择里处仁，便于对子女的教育，故有"孟母三迁"的故事传世。

【译文】

孔子说："选择住处要选在风俗淳美的地方，否则怎么能算明智呢？"

名不正，则言不顺

If names are not rectified, what is said will not sound reasonable.

名不正，则言不顺。

《论语·子路》

If names are not rectified, what is said will not sound reasonable.

【注释】

名不正，则言不顺：子路对孔子说："卫国国君等您去治理政事，您打算首先干什么事?"孔子说："先正名分!"子路不明白，孔子说："名分不正，说话就不能顺理成章；不能顺理成章，事情就办不成；事情办不成，礼乐就不能兴起；礼乐不兴，刑罚就不能得当；刑罚不当，老百姓就无所适从。所以，治理政事必须言出合于礼，能够实行，而不能随随便便。"当时卫国经过父子争夺君位，搞乱了"君臣父子"的名分，所以孔子提出先正名。孔子要正的名，指名分，后来成语"名正言顺"的名，往往指名义而言。

【译文】

孔子说："名分不正，说话就不能顺理成章。"

其身正，不令而行

If the ruler acts properly, the common people will obey him without being ordered to.

其身正，不令而行；其身不正，虽令不从。

《论语·子路》

If the ruler acts properly, the common people will obey him without being ordered to; if the ruler does not act properly, the common people will not obey him even after repeated injunctions.

【注释】

其身正，不令而行： 儒家认为执政者“躬率以正而遇民信也”；“其上不正，遇民不信也”。(《汉书·公孙弘传》)“是故人主之立法，先自为检式仪表，故令行于天下”。(《淮南子·主术》)

【译文】

孔子说:“执政者行为端正，不发命令老百姓也会跟着走；执政者行为不端正，纵三令五申老百姓也不会听从。”

巧言令色

A man who speaks with honeyed words and pretends to be kind cannot be benevolent.

巧言令色，鲜矣仁！

《论语·学而》

A man who speaks with honeyed words and pretends to be kind cannot be benevolent.

【注释】

巧言令色：巧言，花言巧语。令色，伪善，讨好人的表情。朱熹《论语集注》："好其言，善其色，致饰于外，务以悦人，则人欲肆而本正之德亡矣。"《诗经·小雅》巧言篇说："巧言如簧，颜之厚矣。"《尚书·皋陶谟》："何畏乎巧言令色孔壬。"成语"巧言令色"出于此，意为花言巧语，伪装和善，讨好于人。

【译文】

孔子说："一贯花言巧语，伪装和善的人，不会有什么仁德。"

巧言乱德

Sweet words will ruin one's virtue.

巧言乱德。

《论语·卫灵公》

Sweet words will ruin one's virtue.

【注释】

巧言：伪善的言辞；花言巧语。孔子说过："巧言令色，鲜矣仁。"（《论语·学而》）"巧言，令色，足恭，左丘明耻之，丘亦耻之"。（《论语·公冶长》）意为其实并非如此，却花言巧语粉饰之，这是缺乏仁德的表现。程颐："知巧言令色之非仁，则知仁矣。"（《论语解》）

【译文】

孔子说："花言巧语足以败坏道德。"

群居终日，言不及义

Those who spend the whole day long merely chatting idly. . .

群居终日，言不及义，好行小慧，难矣哉！

《论语·卫灵公》

Those who spend the whole day long merely chatting idly, saying unreasonable things and parading their cleverness will accomplish little.

【注释】

北京人把聚在一起闲聊称之为侃大山，热衷此道的人大多无正经事可做，或者不把正经事当正经。闲聊的人因无聊而聚在一起，又没有一定的目的，自然说些言不及义的话。**义**：义理，指事情的道理。鲁迅先生说过："空谈之类，是谈不久，也谈不出什么来的，它终必被事实的镜子照出原形，拖出尾巴而去。"（《鲁迅书简》）

【译文】

孔子说："整天聚在一起闲聊，说话不合道理，好卖弄小聪明，这种人很难有什么成就。"

人而无信，不知其可也

How can one be acceptable without being trustworthy in words?

人而无信，不知其可也。

《论语·为政》

How can one be acceptable without being trustworthy in words?

【注释】

信：孔子伦理思想的范畴之一。处事待人诚实无欺，言行一致的态度是儒家的“五常”之一。孔子将信作为仁的重要体现，他认为诚信是仁人必备的品德。

【译文】

孔子说：“一个人不讲信用，怎么可以立身处世。”

人莫不饮食也

Everyone drinks and eats. . .

人莫不饮食也，鲜能知味也。

《中庸·行明章》

Everyone drinks and eats, but few know the real taste of what has been drunk or eaten.

【注释】

这是孔子感叹中庸之道之所以不能通行天下的原因是因为聪明人太过于明白，认为不足实行；愚笨的人又根本不明白不知道如何实行。他用人人都吃饭喝水却很少有人能品出真正的滋味来作比喻。

【译文】

孔子说："人人都喝水吃饭，却很少有人能品尝出其真正的滋味。"

人无远虑，必有近忧

Worries will soon appear if one gives no thought to a long-term plan.

人无远虑，必有近忧。

《论语·卫灵公》

Worries will soon appear if one gives no thought to a long-term plan.

【注释】

人无远虑，必有近忧：《易传·系辞》："安而不忘危，存而不忘亡，治而不忘乱，是以身安而国家可保也。"

【译文】

孔子说："一个人如果没有长远打算，忧患很快就会出现。"

人一能之，己百之

If others succeed by making one ounce of effort, I will make a hundred times as much effort.

人一能之，己百之。人十能之，己千之。

《中庸·问政章》

If others succeed by making one ounce of effort, I will make a hundred times as much effort; if others succeed by making ten times as much effort, I will make ten hundred times as much effort.

【注释】

中庸：原为《礼记》中的一篇，传为孔子之孙孔伋（子思）所作，朱熹将其从《礼记》中分离出来，独立成书，折衷众说，详为注释，成为《四书》中之一种。朱熹解释说："中者不偏不倚，无过无不及之名；庸，平常也。"又转述二程的话说："不偏之谓中，不易之谓庸，中者天下之正道，庸者天下之定理。"

【译文】

孔子说："别人用一分力气可以做到的，自己要用百分的力气去做。别人用十分力气可以做到的，自己要用千分的力气去做。"

仁者，人也，亲亲为大

Being benevolent means to love people. The greatest benevolence is to love one's own parents.

仁者，人也，亲亲为大。

《中庸·问政章》

Being benevolent means to love people. The greatest benevolence is to love one's own parents.

【注释】

亲亲：爱自己的亲属。本为殷周以来宗法制度之重要内容，后成为儒家伦理思想的组成部分。儒家认为，亲亲是仁的根本。孔子主张“君子笃于亲”，（《论语·泰伯》）孟子认为“亲亲，仁也；敬长，义也”。（《孟子·尽心上》）

【译文】

孔子说：“仁就是爱人的意思，爱自己的父母是最大的仁。”

三军可夺帅也

An army may be deprived of its commanding officer...

三军可夺帅也，匹夫不可夺志也。

《论语·子罕》

An army may be deprived of its commanding officer, yet a man cannot be deprived of his will.

【注释】

三军可夺帅也，匹夫不可夺志也： 孔安国注：“三军虽众，人心不一，则其将帅可夺而取之；匹夫虽微，苟守其志，不可得而夺也。”朱熹注曰：“三军之勇在人，匹夫之志在己。故帅可夺而志不可夺。如可夺，则亦不足谓之志矣。”

【译文】

孔子说：“军队可以丧失主帅，一个人不可丧失志气。”

三人行，必有我师焉

When walking in the company of other men, there must be one I can learn something from.

三人行，必有我师焉。择其善者而从之，其不善者而改之。

《论语·述而》

When walking in the company of other men, there must be one I can learn something from. I shall pick out his merits to follow and his shortcomings for reference to overcome my own.

【注释】

三人行：历代注家对孔子这句名言有不同解释。出入多在“三人行”的“三人”上。朱熹《论语集注》载：“三人同行，其一我也，彼二人者，一善一恶，则我从其善而改其恶。是二人者，皆我师也。”刘宝楠引旧说：“三人之行，本无贤愚。其有善有不善者，皆随事所见，择而从之改之。非谓一人善，一人不善也。即从其善，即是我师。”（《论语正义》）卫国大夫公孙朝曾问子贡：“你老师（孔子）的学问是跟谁学的？”子贡说他并没有固定的老师，而是无处不学习。子贡的话才是孔子这句名言的正确解释。

【译文】

孔子说：“有几个人一起走路，其中便一定有值得我学习的人。我选取那些优点而学习，看出那些缺点而检查改正。”

士不可以不弘毅

A scholar must be resolute and steadfast. . .

士不可以不弘毅，任重而道远。仁以为己任，不亦重乎？死而后已，不亦远乎？

《论语·泰伯》

Zeng Zi said, "A scholar must be resolute and steadfast, for his burden is heavy and his road is long. To practice the virtue of benevolence in the world is his burden. Is that not heavy? Only with death does his journey come to an end. Is that not long?"

【注释】

士：商、西周、春秋时最低级的贵族阶层。春秋时多为卿大夫家臣，有的士食田，有的士食俸禄，春秋末成为统治阶级中知识分子的通称。孔子即属于这个阶层。
弘毅：抱负远大，意志坚强。

【译文】

曾子说："读书人要刚强而有毅力，因为他们肩负重任而前程远大。以实现仁德于天下，这担子还不重吗？为此目的，至死方休，这还不遥远吗？"

士见危致命，见得思义

It is satisfactory for a gentleman to lay down his life. . .

士见危致命，见得思义。

《论语·子张》

Zi Zhang said, "It is satisfactory for a gentleman to lay down his life when his country is in danger, and to keep in mind what is right in the face of gain."

【注释】

见危致命：国家遇到危难时肯献出生命。和《论语·宪问》中的“见危授命”意思同。**见得思义**：北宋邢昺解释说：“见得思义者，言若有所得，当思义然后取，不可苟也。”（《论语正义》疏）

【译文】

子张说：“读书人遇到国家危难时肯献出生命，不轻取不义之财。”

逝者如斯夫，不舍昼夜

"Time is going on like this river, flowing away endlessly day and night."

逝者如斯夫！不舍昼夜。

《论语·子罕》

Standing by the side of a river, Confucius sighed, "Time is going on like this river, flowing away endlessly day and night."

【注释】

逝：流去。孔子是一个“学而不厌”的人，爱学习的人，才知道珍惜光阴。孔子看着奔流不息的河水首先感叹时光流失，竟不知不觉“老之将至”，而自己一生虽然抱着积极的态度参与社会改革，而现实却是每况愈下，自己恢复西周的理想不能实现了，他不禁感叹说：“我老了，已经很长时间没有梦见周公了。”（《论语·述而》）

【译文】

孔子站在河边感叹道：“过去的时光就像这河水一样，日夜不停地流去。”

岁寒，然后知松柏之后凋也

Only when the weather turns cold can we see that the leaves of pines and cypresses are the last to wither and fall.

岁寒，然后知松柏之后凋也。

《论语·子罕》

Only when the weather turns cold can we see that the leaves of pines and cypresses are the last to wither and fall.

【注释】

松柏：喻栋梁之材。荀子把松柏喻君子。“岁不寒无以知松柏；事不难无以知君子。”朱熹引谢上蔡注曰：“士穷见节义，世乱识忠臣。”**凋**：凋谢。

【译文】

孔子说：“到了严寒的季节，才知道松柏树是不落叶的。”

为政以德

He who rules his state on a moral basis would be supported by the people. . .

为政以德，譬如北辰居其所而群星共之。

《论语·为政》

He who rules his state on a moral basis would be supported by the people, just as the Polar Star is encircled by all the other stars.

【注释】

为政以德：孔子主张德治，他说："道之以政，齐之以刑，民免而无耻；道之以德，齐之以礼，有耻且格。"（《论语·为政》）孔子认为政、刑只能使人不敢犯罪，德、礼才能使人知耻归心。

【译文】

孔子说："执政者如果用道德来治理国政，自己就会像北极星受群星环绕一样受到百姓们的拥护。"

温故而知新

If one is able to acquire new knowledge by reviewing old knowledge. . .

温故而知新，可以为师矣。

《论语·为政》

If one is able to acquire new knowledge by reviewing old knowledge, he is qualified to be a tutor.

【注释】

温故而知新："温故"，即温习已学过的知识；"知新"，即获得新的知识。"而"有并列与推出两种意义。温习已学过的知识，从中获得新知识是孔子的教育方法，也是他对弟子们的要求。他认为能做到这一点无疑就可以当老师了。

【译文】

孔子说："温习学过的知识时，能从中获得新知识的人，就可以做老师了。"

我非生而知之者

I was not born with knowledge. . .

我非生而知之者，好古，敏以求之者也。

《论语·述而》

I was not born with knowledge, but, being fond of ancient culture, I was eager to seek it through diligence.

【注释】

生而知之者：孔子把人分为生而知之者、学而知之者、困而学之者、困而不学者四等。在知识来源上，则认为只有“生而知之”和“学而知之”两种。他把“生而知之者”列为上等人，但他说自己并不是“生而知之者”而是“学而知之者”。
敏：敏捷，勤敏。

【译文】

孔子说：“我不是生来就有知识的人，而是由于爱好古代文化，靠了勤奋和敏捷求得知识的。”

吾日三省吾身

Every day I examine myself once and again. . .

吾日三省吾身：为人谋而不忠乎？与朋友交而不信乎？传不习乎？

《论语·学而》

Zeng Zi(a disciple of Confucius') said, "Every day I examine myself once and again: Have I tried my utmost to help others? Have I been honest to my friends? Have I diligently reviewed the instructions from the Master?"

【注释】

三省："三"，次数多，并不一定是确指三。省（xǐng），自我检查，反省，内省。表示再三反省自身。**忠**：忠诚。**信**：诚信。**传**（chuán）：动词作名词用，老师的传授。**习**：温习，实习，复习。

【译文】

曾子说："我每天都再三反省自己：为别人办事是否尽心竭力了呢？同朋友交往是否以诚相待了呢？老师教的功课是否用心复习了呢？"

吾十有五而志于学

Since the age of fifteen, I have devoted myself to learning...

吾十有五而志于学，三十而立，四十而不惑，五十而知天命，六十而耳顺，七十而从心所欲，不逾矩。

《论语·为政》

Confucius said, "Since the age of fifteen, I have devoted myself to learning; since thirty, I have been well established; since forty, I have understood many things and have no longer been confused; since fifty, I have known my heaven-sent duty; since sixty, I have been able to distinguish right and wrong in other people's words; and since seventy, I have been able to do what I intend freely without breaking the rules."

【注释】

志于学：孔子说："吾十有五而志于学"。意谓孔子十五岁开始学习做官所必须的礼乐知识，至于向谁学习和学习的具体内容古书记载不多。**而立、不惑、天命、耳顺**：从此以后成为三十岁、四十岁、五十岁、六十岁的代称。

【译文】

孔子说："我十五岁有志于做学问。三十岁立身处世站稳了脚跟；四十岁掌握了各种知识遇事不迷惑；五十岁知道上天赋予自己的使命；六十岁对别人的话能辨别是非曲直；七十岁既使随心所欲也不会有越规的行为。"

无欲速，无见小利

Do not make haste; do not covet small gains.

做事不要图快，不要贪图小利。一味图快反而达不到目的，贪图小利就办不成大事。

无欲速，无见小利。欲速则不达，见小利则大事不成。

《论语·子路》

Do not make haste; do not covet small gains. If you make haste, you cannot reach your goal; if you covet small gains, your efforts will not culminate in great achievements.

【注释】

无欲速，无见小利：子夏做了莒父县长官，向孔子请教如何管理政事，孔子说了上面的话。子夏即卜商（前507—?）孔子弟子。姓卜，名商，字子夏。春秋末魏（一说卫）国人，少孔子四十四岁。在孔门弟子中以“文学”著称，才思敏捷。他主张“学而优则仕”。(《论语·子张》）孔子死后，他到魏国讲学，并为“魏文侯师”。(《史记·仲尼弟子列传》)

【译文】

孔子说:“做事不要图快，不要贪图小利。一味图快反而达不到目的，贪图小利就办不成大事。”

小不忍，则乱大谋

Lack of patience in small matters will bring destruction to overall plans.

小不忍，则乱大谋。

《论语·卫灵公》

Lack of patience in small matters will bring destruction to overall plans.

【注释】

小不忍："小"包括"小忿怒"和"小仁小惠"两个意思。朱熹《论语集注》："小不忍，如妇人之仁，匹夫之勇皆是。"又说："妇人之仁，不能忍于爱；匹夫之勇，不能忍于忿，皆能乱大谋。"

【译文】

孔子说："小事上不能忍耐，就会坏了大事。"

性相近也，习相远也

Men are similar to one another by nature. They diverge gradually as a result of different customs.

性相近也，习相远也。

《论语·阳货》

Men are similar to one another by nature. They diverge gradually as a result of different customs.

【注释】

性相近也，习相远也：孔子的人性观，孔子认为人性是共似的，并没有善恶之分，只是由于后来生存环境的不同而有所改变罢了。后来孟子则持“性善”说，“人性之善也，犹水之就下也。”（《孟子·告子上》）《三字经》曰：“人之初，性本善。性相近，习相远。”就是从这里套用而来。

【译文】

孔子说：“人的本性都差不多，只是由于习俗不同，便相距越来越远了。”

学而不思则罔

It throws one into bewilderment to read without thinking...

只读书不思考，就不会分析。只空想不读书，就不明事理。

学而不思则罔，思而不学则殆。

《论语·为政》

It throws one into bewilderment to read without thinking whereas it places one in jeopardy to think without reading.

【注释】

罔（wǎng）：迷惘，蒙蔽。“学而不思”则容易受欺骗。**殆**（dài）：《论语》中的“殆”有两个意思。一，疑惑，“多见阙殆。”（《论语·为政》）二，危险，“今之从政者殆而”。（《论语·微子》）

【译文】

孔子说：“只读书不思考，就不会分析。只空想不读书，就不明事理。”

学而不厌，悔人不倦

Study hard and never feel contented, and never be tired of teaching others.

学而不厌，悔人不倦。

《论语·述而》

Study hard and never feel contented, and never be tired of teaching others.

【注释】

学而不厌，悔人不倦：好学而不厌，教诲别人而不知疲倦表现了孔子于求知学问的勤勉不怠和教授弟子的一腔热忱，这也是孔子对“学”与“教”的认识。

【译文】

孔子说：“学习努力而不满足，教导别人不知疲倦。”

学而时习之，不亦说乎

“Is it not a pleasure after all to practice in due time what one has learnt?

学而时习之，不亦说乎？有朋自远方来，不亦乐乎？人不知，而不愠，不亦君子乎？

《论语·学而》

Confucius said,"Is it not a pleasure after all to practice in due time what one has learnt? Is it not a delight after all to have friends come from afar? Is it not a gentleman after all who will not take offence when others fail to appreciate him?"

【注释】

时：作"以时"（一定的时候；适当的时候）或"时常"解。**习**：一般作温习解，在古书中也有"实习"、"演习"的意思。**说**：读悦（yuè），高兴、愉快的意思。**《学而》**：为《论语》首篇。《论语》本无篇名，是后人选每篇第一章前两个字（个别选三个字）作篇名。朱熹《论语集注》曰：此"乃入道之门，积德之基，学者之先务也。"**有朋**：旧注曰："同门曰朋。"这里的"朋"当指弟子解。《史记·孔子世家》："故孔子不仕，退而修诗、书、礼乐，弟子弥众，至自远方。"

【译文】

孔子说："对学过的知识按时去实习它，不也是很好的事吗？有朋友从远方来，不是很快乐的事吗？不为别人不了解自己而抱怨，不是很有修养的君子风度吗？

言顾行，行顾言

When a man speaks, he should think of his acts; when he acts, he should think of what he said.

言顾行，行顾言。

《中庸·不远章》

When a man speaks, he should think of his acts; when he acts, he should think of what he said.

【注释】

言顾行，行顾言：言，言论。行，行为，实践。孔子主张言行并重、言行一致。他说："君子名之必可言也，言之必可行也。君子于其言，无所苟而已矣。"（《论语·子路》）考察一个人，他主张"听其言而观其行"。他甚至主张行重于言，他认为"有德者必有言，有言者不必有德"。（《论语·宪问》）他曾对子贡说："先行其言而后从之。"他反对说大话，空话。他认为"巧言乱德"。

【译文】

孔子说："说话要照顾到行动，行动要照顾到说话。"

一张一弛，文武之道也

The principle of kings Wen and Wu was to alternate tension with relaxation.

一张一弛，文武之道也。

《礼记·杂记下》

The principle of kings Wen and Wu was to alternate tension with relaxation.

【注释】

孔子仕鲁期间有一次参加蜡祭活动。孔子问一同观蜡的子贡："赐也，乐乎?"子贡答："一国之人，皆若狂，赐未知其乐也。"孔子说："张而不弛，文武弗能也；弛而不张，文武弗为也。一张一弛，文武之道也。"（《礼记·杂记下》）蜡祭，古代腊月祭祀百神的活动。子贡对老百姓在节日里狂欢的情绪很不理解，孔子的意思是说：老百姓辛苦一年，利用节日娱乐休息一下是可以理解的。

【译文】

孔子说："有紧有松，才是周文王、武王治理国家的办法。"

益者三乐，损者三乐

There are three kinds of beneficial pleasure. Equally there are three kinds of harmful pleasure.

益者三乐，损者三乐。乐节礼乐，乐道人之善，乐多贤友，益矣。乐骄乐，乐佚游，乐宴乐，损矣。"

《论语·季氏》

There are three kinds of beneficial pleasure. Equally there are three kinds of harmful pleasure. The three beneficial kinds include: to prepare for the rites and music; to give publicity to others' good qualities; to make friends with those who are virtuous. The three harmful kinds are as follows: to be arrogant about one's position; to loiter to one's heart's content; and to indulge in food and drink.

【注释】

益者三乐，损者三乐：孔子认为以得到礼乐的调节为快乐，以宣扬别人的长处为快乐，以多交贤良的朋友为快乐，这是有益的快乐。以尊贵骄傲为快乐。以尽情游荡为快乐，以吃吃喝喝为快乐，这是有害的快乐。宋·苏轼说过："天下之乐无穷，而以适意为悦。"人有各种各样的快乐，孔子把快乐分为有益和有害的各三种。

【译文】

孔子说："有益的快乐有三种，有害的快乐也有三种。以得到礼乐的调节为快乐，以宣扬别人的长处为快乐，以多交贤良的朋友为快乐，这是有益的快乐。以尊贵骄傲为快乐，以尽情游荡为快乐，以吃吃喝喝为快乐，这是有害的快乐。"

益者三友，损者三友

There are three kinds of people one may make friends with. Equally, there are three kinds of people one should not make friends with.

益者三友，损者三友。友直，友谅，友多闻，益矣。友便辟，友善柔，友便佞，损矣。

《论语·季氏》

There are three kinds of people one may make friends with. Equally, there are three kinds of people one should not make friends with. It is beneficial for one to make friends with those who are upright, honest, and erudite. It is harmful for one to make friends with those who toady, those who flatter people but slander them behind their backs, those who brag but are not erudite at all.

【注释】

益者、损者： 益，利益，好处。损，伤害。孔子认为同正直的人、诚实的人、广见博闻的人交朋友，是有益的。同谄媚奉承的人、当面恭维背后毁谤的人、夸夸其谈并无真才实学的人交朋友，是有害的。

【译文】

孔子说："交朋友有三种人可以交，有三种人不可以交。同正直的人、诚实的人、广见博闻的人交朋友，是有益的。同谄媚奉承的人、当面恭维背后毁谤的人、夸夸其谈并无真才实学的人交朋友，是有害的。"

有德者必有言

A virtuous man must have said something of note.

有德者必有言，有言者不必有德。

《论语·宪问》

A virtuous man must have said something of note; but someone who has said something of note is not necessarily a man of virtue.

【注释】

德：古“德”与“得”字相通。孔子将“德”阐发成儒家的伦理范畴，专指道德、品德。孔子所说的德内容包括仁、义、孝、弟、忠、恕、让、信、中庸等。**言：**有益的话。

【译文】

孔子说：“道德高尚的人一定会有有益的名言传世，但有名言传世的人不一定都是道德高尚的人。”

有教无类

In educating people, I treat everyone the same.

有教无类。

《论语·卫灵公》

In educating people, I treat everyone the same.

Note: This could also be translated as: "Everyone is entitled to be educated."

【注释】

有教无类：孔子对教育的主张，意即教育不分种类。何晏注疏："类，谓种类。言人所在见教，无有贵贱种类也。"皇侃疏："人乃有贵贱，宜同资教，不可以其种类、庶鄙而不教之也。"也有把类解释成"善恶之殊"，似不合孔子本意。孔子主张"自行束脩以上，吾未尝无诲焉"（《论语·述而》），孔门弟子中有拥有很大权力和财富的贵族子弟，又有家境贫寒的平民百姓；既有富商大贾，又有体力劳动者，甚至还有盗者。故有人认为孔门多杂。

【译文】

孔子说："我对凡来求学的人，都无区别地加以教育。"

愚而好自用

A foolish man likes to think himself clever...

愚而好自用，贱而好自专。

《中庸·自用章》

A foolish man likes to think himself clever and a man in low post likes to take liberties to make decisions on his own.

【注释】

自用：自以为是，恃自己的聪明才力行事。**自专**：只凭个人意见而独断专行。

【译文】

孔子说："愚笨的人却喜欢自作聪明，卑贱的人却喜欢自作主张。"

朝闻道，夕死可矣

If one learns the truth in the morning, one would never regret dying the same evening.

朝闻道，夕死可矣。

《论语·里仁》

If one learns the truth in the morning, one would never regret dying the same evening.

【注释】

闻道：指对真理的得知，把握。宋·朱熹《论语集注》：“道者，事物当然之理。苟得闻之，则生顺死安，无复遗恨矣。”顾炎武《日知录》卷七：“吾见其进也，未见其止也。有一日未死之身，则有一日未闻之道。”意即“生命不息，学习不止”。

【译文】

孔子说：“早晨学得真理，当天晚上死掉也不后悔。”

知之为知之，不知为不知

If you understand what you learn, say you do; if not, say you do not.

知之为知之，不知为不知，是知也。

《论语·为政》

If you understand what you learn, say you do; if not, say you do not. Only then are you an intelligent man.

【注释】

知之为知之，不知为不知：这是孔子对仲由说的话。仲由（前542—前480）孔子弟子。姓仲，名由，字子路，一字季路。春秋末鲁国人，少孔子九岁。出身贫贱，为孔门弟子中年龄较长者。性耿直好勇。敬重孔子并常直率提出不同意见。**知**（zhì）：同“智”。

【译文】

孔子说：“懂就说懂，不懂就说不懂，才是聪明人。”

知之者不如好之者

To be fond of knowledge is better than merely to acquire it.

知之者不如好之者，好之者不如乐之者。

《论语·雍也》

To be fond of knowledge is better than merely to acquire it; to take delight in it is still better than merely to be fond of it.

【注释】

知：知道、懂得。**好**：爱好，喜好。**乐**：快乐。知之者，好之者，乐之者，对这三种对待学业不同态度的人。孔子赞成后者。他本人就是一个以从事学业为快乐的人。他说自己是一个“发愤忘食，乐以忘忧，不知老之将至”的人。（《论语·述而》）

【译文】

孔子说：“懂得学业的人不如喜爱学业的人，喜爱学业的人不如以从事学业为快乐的人。”

知者不惑，仁者不忧

A wise man is never cheated, a virtuous man is never worried...

知者不惑，仁者不忧，勇者不惧。

《论语·子罕》

A wise man is never cheated, a virtuous man is never worried and a courageous man is never afraid.

【注释】

知、仁、勇：孔子认为“知仁勇三者，天下之达德也。”（《中庸·问政章》）达德，即天下共通的大德。可见孔子对知仁勇这三种品德的看重。《论语正义》引《申鉴·杂言下》注曰：“君子乐天知命故不忧；审物明辨故不惑；定心致公故不惧。”孔子自谦其不具备这君子必备的三达德，而子贡则认为老师已然是“三达德”的化身了。

【译文】

孔子说：“聪明人不受欺骗，品德高尚的人没有忧虑，勇敢的人无所畏惧。”

知者不失人，亦不失言

A wise man shall not let a man slip into uselessness, nor shall he waste his words.

知者不失人，亦不失言。

《论语·卫灵公》

A wise man shall not let a man slip into uselessness, nor shall he waste his words.

【注释】

失人、失言：孔子说："对可以交往的人而不与之交往，是错失了人；对不可以交谈的人而与之交谈，是失言。"他认为只有聪明人（知者）才能做到既不失人又不失言。

【译文】

孔子说："聪明人不会失人，也不会失言。"

知者乐水，仁者乐山

The wise take delight in water, the benevolent in mountains.

知者乐水，仁者乐山。知者动，仁者静。知者乐，仁者寿。

《论语·雍也》

The wise take delight in water, the benevolent in mountains. The wise are active while the benevolent are still. The wise enjoy life while the benevolent achieve longevity.

【注释】

知者乐水，仁者乐山：这是孔子关于自然美的思想。孔子认为君子在人格修养上各有侧重，人们的精神品质不同，对自然山水的喜爱也不相同。自然的山和水，各有动人之处，人的精神品质也各有侧重。仁者所以喜欢山是因为山有静养万物的宽厚博大，而仁者正因为宽厚沉稳所以才能“不忧”，是故仁者爱山。水的活泼生动，奔流不息，正为思维敏捷善于应对的智者所喜爱，是为“不惑”。孔子爱山却更爱水。

【译文】

孔子说：“聪明人喜欢水，有仁德的人喜爱山。聪明人好动，有仁德的人好静。聪明人生活快乐，有仁德的人能享高寿。”

志士仁人，无求生以害仁

A man of benevolence and lofty ideals should not, at the expense of benevolence, cling cravenly to life instead of braving death.

志士仁人，无求生以害仁，有杀身以成仁。

《论语·卫灵公》

A man of benevolence and lofty ideals should not, at the expense of benevolence, cling cravenly to life instead of braving death. He will, on the contrary, lay down his life for the accomplishment of benevolence.

【注释】

志士仁人：有节操，公而忘私的人。**杀身成仁**：为了成全仁德，可以不顾自己的生命。后多指为维护正义事业而牺牲生命。

【译文】

孔子说："志士仁人，没有贪生怕死而损害仁德的，只有牺牲自己而成全仁德。"

志于道，据于德

Stick to the way to your goal, base yourself on virtue.

志于道，据于德，依于仁，游于艺。

《论语·述而》

Stick to the way to your goal, base yourself on virtue, lean upon benevolence, and take your recreation in the six arts(i. e. music, the rites, archery, carriage driving, classic books and arithmetic).

【注释】

志于道：孔子提出的读书人应具备的一种立志追求真理的精神。**据于德**：以道德为根据。朱熹解“据”为“执守之意”，“德”为“得”，意即“得其道于心而不失”。**依于仁**：以仁道为凭藉。**游于艺**：指六艺（礼、乐、射、御、书、数），还有一说指《礼》、《乐》、《书》、《诗》、《易》、《春秋》，即六经。是孔子教育学生的六门功课。

【译文】

孔子说：“志向在道，根据在德，依靠在仁，游习于六艺之中。”

质胜文则野，文胜质则史

One would seem uncouth with more simplicity than refinement, and seem superficial with more refinement than simplicity.

质胜文则野，文胜质则史。文质彬彬，然后君子。

《论语·雍也》

One would seem uncouth with more simplicity than refinement, and seem superficial with more refinement than simplicity. Only when these two qualities are well-balanced can one become a real gentleman.

【注释】

文：在《论语》里“文”字有多种含义，此处“文”为孔子论述艺术形式与内容关系的审美范畴。作文彩解。**野**：意指粗野、鄙俗。**史**：虚华无实。**文质彬彬**：彬彬，形容配合谐调。孔子认为“质”和“文”相配谐调，才是作人（君子）的标准。后来这个成语在流行中多用以形容人举止文雅，态度端正从容。唐·王勃《三国论》：“文帝富于春秋，光膺禅让，临朝恭俭，博览坟籍，文质彬彬，庶几君子者矣。”

【译文】

孔子说：“一个人朴实多于文彩，就未免显得粗俗，如果文彩多于朴实，就未免显得虚浮，文彩和朴实配合适当，这才是君子风度。”

中人以上，可以语上也

Advanced knowledge can be transmitted to those who are above the average. . .

中人以上，可以语上也；中人以下，不可以语上也。

《论语·雍也》

Advanced knowledge can be transmitted to those who are above the average, but never to those who are below the average.

【注释】

中人：孔子曾把人分为四等“生而知之者上也，学而知之者次也；困而学之，又其次也；困而不学，民斯为下矣。”（《论语·季氏》）这里的“中人”，显然是指“学而知之”的人。孔子虽然把“生而知之”的人列为上等人，但他又说“我非生而知之者，好古，敏以求之者也。”（《论语·述而》）实际上他并不认为真有“生而知之”的人。**上**：高深的知识。

【译文】

孔子说：“对具有中等接受水平以上的人，可以传授高深知识；对中等水平以下的人，不可以传授高深知识。”

主忠信，无友不如己者

A gentleman should pay great attention to loyalty and sincerity, and not make close friends with those whose morality is inferior to his.

主忠信，无友不如己者。过则勿惮改。

《论语·学而》

A gentleman should pay great attention to loyalty and sincerity, and not make close friends with those whose morality is inferior to his. If he makes a mistake, he should not be afraid of correcting it.

【注释】

主忠信：忠和信都是孔子的伦理道德范畴。**无友不如己者**：对孔子这句话历来有不同的解释。一说不结交比自己差的朋友；一说每个朋友身上都有自己没有的长处。**惮**（dàn）：畏惧。

【译文】

孔子说："要重道德，慎交友，有过错，随时改正。"

自古皆有死，民无信不立

Man has been destined to die since time immemorial. But if people lose their trust in the government then the country has lost its basis.

自古以来,人都会死的。如果失去人民对政府的信任这一项,也就失去了立国之本了。

自古皆有死，民无信不立。

《论语·颜渊》

Man has been destined to die since time immemorial. But if people lose their trust in the government then the country has lost its basis.

【注释】

子贡问怎样治理国家，孔子说："粮食充足，军备充足，人民信任政府。"子贡问："如果迫不得已一定要去掉一项，在这三项中先去掉哪一项？"孔子说："去掉军备。"子贡又说："如果迫不得已还要去掉一项，在这二项中该去掉哪一项？"孔子说："去掉粮食。没有粮食，虽然会饿死，但自古以来，人都会死的。如果失去人民对政府的信任这一项，也就失去了立国之本了。"孔子的话反映了儒家的民本思想。

【译文】

孔子说："自古以来，人都会死的。如果失去人民对政府的信任这一项，也就失去了立国之本了。"

图书在版编目（CIP）数据

孔子说 / 蔡希勤编注. －北京：华语教学出版社，2006
（中国圣人文化丛书. 老人家说系列）
ISBN 978-7-80200-211-1

I. 孔... II. 蔡... III. 汉语－对外汉语教学－语言读物 IV. H195.5

中国版本图书馆 CIP 数据核字 (2006) 第 071762 号

出版人：单　瑛
责任编辑：韩　晖　　封面设计：胡　湖
印刷监制：佟汉冬　　绘　　图：李士伋

老人家说 · 孔子说
蔡希勤　编注
*

华语教学出版社出版
（中国北京百万庄大街 24 号　邮政编码 100037）
电话: 010-68320585
传真: 010-68326333
网址：www.sinolingua.com.cn
电子信箱: fxb@sinolingua.com.cn
北京松源印刷有限公司印刷
中国国际图书贸易总公司海外发行
（中国北京车公庄西路 35 号）
北京邮政信箱第 399 号　邮政编码 100044
新华书店国内发行
2004年（大32开）第一版
2009 年第二次印刷
(汉英)
ISBN 978-7-80200-211-1
9-CE-3728P
定价：29.80 元